Fishing with My Papaw

By Alvin D. Walker Jr.
Illustrated By Hicham Badari

This Book Belong To:

My Name: _____

My Address: _____

Your Phone Number: _____

Dedication

I want to dedicate this heart- felt children's book to my grandkids; Angel, Angela, Jón Jon, Sparkle, Tee Two, Brooklynn and Bella, and Avery

Love You,
Papaw

About the Author

I am one happy grandfather, who has been blessed with some wonderful grandkids.

(Digital online)

ISBN: 978-1-7378051-9-9 (Paperback)

ISBN: 978-0-57836309-7 (Hardcover)

Library of Congress Control Number: public record Walker, Alvin

Any references to historical events, real people, or real places are used fictitiously. Names, characters, and places are products of the author's imagination.

Front cover image by Hicham Badari Images by Hicham Badari

Illustrated By Hicham Badari

Printed in the United States of America. First printing edition 2022.

Publisher by Alvin Walker

Contact Info: https://www.amazon.com/author/alvinwalker.com

Table of Contents

Introduction

I love to go fishing with my Papaw. We have so much fun being outdoors surrounded by nature. Discovering all the little creatures at the pond like; turtles, frogs, snakes, tadpoles, lizards, and birds. There are also larger animals such as; rabbits, foxes, armadillos, deer, buzzards, and coyotes. Papaw tells me about the animals he has seen at the pond and something about them.

Chapter 1: Preparing for the Fishing Trip

My Papaw and I prepare for two days; before the fishing trip. We clean and oil all the fishing rods and reels. We go to the store to buy all the snacks such as; soda, potato chips, cookies, twinkies, and summer sausage.

Chapter 2: Waking up at 5:00 in the Morning

The day of the fishing trip, we got up at 5:00 in the morning. I was so sleepy, I could barely stay awake, but I was so excited about fishing.

I was walking around like a zombie.

Chapter 3: Papaw Telling Tall Tales at Breakfast

At breakfast, Papaw talks about massive fish he caught and the ones that got away. I was thinking about the fishes that I would catch on the trip. Will the fish be green with dark green bands on its side and have a really big mouth? Will the fish have whiskers and be black in color?

Will they have small mouths with short heads with blue dots on them?

Chapter 4: Traveling to the Honey Hole

After we pack up the truck, we are off to the bait shop to pick up fishing bait. We fish with worms, minnows and shrimp. Papaw has a bucket with a box on it that blows bubbles to keep the minnows alive. The worms and shrimp are kept cool in the cooler.

Chapter 5: Arriving at a Beautiful Pond in the Country

After about half an hour of driving that seemed like three hours. We arrive at the pond. It is beautiful. The water looks like glass and is crystal clear. It is the fall, and the trees have so many colors. The fish are jumping on the sides around the algae plants.

Chapter 6: Locating a Good Place to Fish at the Pond

We walk around the pond to look for a good area to fish and place the fishing supplies. We decide underneath a tree at the corner of the pond would be the best place. It is a place where algae plants are thick, but not so thick you'll get your line hung up. It's where the bait fishes can hide from the bigger fish. Papaw said the big fish tend to hang around the algae bed and ambush the smaller fish.

Chapter 7: Putting the Bait on the Hook

Now, here comes the nasty part putting the bait on the hook. We start with minnows as the bait to use, because it is a native bait from the pond. The minnows are alive, so they are moving, and they attract the bass and large fish to bite. Papaw shows me how to put the minnow onto the hook. He says to hook the minnow through the top part of the mouth, so it will stay alive on the hook. Then I bait the line up and put a fishing bobber on it. I set it for about four feet deep and throw the line out into the pond.

Chapter 8: Start Catching Fish "Fish On!"

Within a few minutes the fishing bobber starts dancing around; then goes under the water. Papaw tells me to set the hook, so I pull back. The fish is on and I start reeling the fish into the bank. The fish jump into the air. It is a bass, and it is a big one! I am trying to reel it in as fast as I can, but the fish pulls harder, taking out more drag. Papaw says, "Take it easy", "Take your time so the fish won't break the line".

I listen to my Papaw and take my time reeling the fish into the bank.

I get the fish off of hook and hold him up. "Wow" I said. Then I put him into the fish basket and into the water to keep him alive.

I then put another minnow back onto my line and throw it into the water. After a little wait, the bobber starts traveling across the pond toward the deep part.

Papaw yells, "Set the hook".

So, I pull back on the fishing rod. The fishing rod is bending a lot, and whatever is on the other end is heavy. This one is different from the last one. It does not jump, it just pulls. When I finally get it close to the bank, I see it is a huge catfish! Papaw has to take him off the hook for me, because he has sharp fins on the side and the top that may stick me.

Papaw takes the fish off the hook and put into the fish basket, then puts it back into the water.

Chapter 9: Catch of the Day; a "Big Old Bass" and a "Big Old Catfish"

The rest of the day it is one fish after another. All diverse types from perch and bass, to channel cat and crappie. The fish are all varied sizes, from small to medium to large. The small and large fish are released back into the pond. We keep a few of the medium fish to cook for dinner and release the rest back into the pond. Papaw says by doing this, we will always have good fishing at the pond. The high lights of the day are an eight pounds bass and a twenty-four pounds channel catfish.

Chapter 10: This is the Part Where no one Wants to Go Home

Papaw says it is getting a little late and we better start loading up to go home. I move as slowly as I possibly can. The whole time I "am gathering and loading up stuff onto the truck. I' am looking at the pond to see if fish are jumping or if anything is moving around in the pond.

I look at Papaw and ask, "When are we coming back?" He answers, "Soon, soon".

Conclusion:

A big part of everyone's life is for an older family member to pass on knowledge and skills to a younger family member. It is a part of our social interactions. It is also part of our family bonding and of caring for each other in the family and experiencing doing things together.

The End

"Good Fishing"

"Fish ON"

www.ingramcontent.com/pod-product-compliance
Lightning Source LLC
Chambersburg PA
CBHW051348290326
41933CB00042B/3338